Winning Interview

About the Author
John Lee Tozzi

Mr. Tozzi has more than thirty years of experience as a leader in education and training. He has interviewed hundreds of job candidates using a variety of interviewing models. During this time, he observed the behaviors and characteristics of the winning candidates. Subsequently, he founded the company, Winning Interview / winninginterview.com, which has successfully helped clients from a range of careers attain the jobs they were seeking.

- All Rights Reserved –

ISBN: 1448646200
EAN-13 is 9781448646203

Winning Interview
Showcase Your Talents!

Table of Contents

Chapter I
Let's Get Started

Our Mission – To Empower You

The mission of *Winning Interview* is to empower you to communicate your knowledge, demonstrate your skills, and showcase your talents during a job interview.

Introduction

The many interview preparation books that are currently available offer sample answers to typical questions and advice about dress, grooming, and punctuality. *Winning Interview* is different. It is an innovative and effective approach to successful interviewing.

Obviously, the purpose of an interview is to give an employer the opportunity to select the most qualified person among a field of candidates. What is important to realize is that the resume and screening procedures used by employers often result in a list of interview candidates who are all capable of fulfilling the responsibilities of the job. Typically, these candidates arrive on time, are well-groomed, and are appropriately dressed - givens. If they truly are serious about competing for the job, they also have thoughtfully prepared responses to potential questions. Any one of them could win the interview, and then do the job.

What then distinguishes the candidate who is selected? Experience? Degrees? *Winning Interview* maintains that in most situations the successful candidate is determined by a combination of nine factors, the *Winning Interview 9*. These nine factors are personal traits that you can learn to communicate during an interview. The *Winning Interview 9* are the substance of this book. The goal is to help you understand these nine factors, realize their importance, and then effectively project them during your interview.

A Clear and Concise Method

This book is designed for job candidates who are motivated to interview successfully. It leads you beyond the mentality of preparing for a job interview by merely reviewing potential questions and dressing for success. Instead, *Winning Interview* offers concise and well-organized explanations of interviewing strategies that transcend the common notion of interview preparation. The rationales and key concepts are presented clearly and succinctly. The book is deliberately designed to be a substantive, but quick read. It leads you to coach yourself through several mock interviews that you video record. In turn, you are provided with charts and assessment procedures for analyzing and evaluating your mock interviews. These tools provide you with a methodology for moving beyond simply answering questions and dressing well to a level of performance that can empower you to distinguish yourself as the most outstanding candidate, the one who wins the interview. The process also gives you a starting point, a clear direction for interview preparation, and leads you to *get ready to be ready*.

Is This Book for You? Business, Sales, Medicine, CEO, Technical Specialist

This *Winning Interview* process has developed as an outcome of many years of observing and evaluating candidates during job interviews. It also is an outgrowth of the *winninginterview.com* company which has helped candidates successfully attain jobs ranging from lumber sales, to marine engineering management, to educational administration, to telecommunication CEO. The process is effective regardless of the content of the interview, whether the field is journalism, technology, medicine, business, sales, or education, and identifies critical interviewing strategies that can empower candidates to win their interviews for any career.

The Layout of This Book: Leading You Step-by-Step to Success

Winning Interview presents a logical and sequential process that leads you to prepare for your interview. One of your initial tasks is to learn about various interview formats. As your understanding of the formats grows, so will your confidence and effectiveness in dealing with them. Next, *Winning Interview* briefly highlights interviewing basics, ranging from references to punctuality to appropriate dress. However, the book assumes that these interview basics are givens, and unlike other interview preparation books that devote the bulk of their content to these topics, *Winning Interview* provides only cursory overviews and checklists.

Integrated throughout the book are defined tasks for you to complete. One of these leads you to create and conduct a mock interview for the job you are seeking. You video record your performance in that interview. This initial video recording is your *cold interview*. It represents your performance before you study and master the critical components of the *Winning Interview* process. These components are the key to your success and are called the *Winning Interview 9*.

The next section of the book introduces the *Winning Interview 9* and begins with the central focus in most interview preparation training: effectively responding to questions. Surely excellent responses are critical for a successful job interview; for that reason, the *Winning Interview* preparation process provides considerable attention to helping you develop strong responses. Nevertheless, to be the winning candidate, you must transcend the typical mentality of: *I will be prepared to do a good job of answering questions.* Therefore, the subsequent content of the book leads you one-by-one through eight additional factors that can distinguish you as the successful candidate and help you win your interview. As you gain an understanding of these nine critical factors, the *Winning Interview 9*, you will lay the groundwork for increasing your competence for your upcoming interview.

Next, you will use rating sheets based on the *Winning Interview 9* as you watch sample interview responses available on *winninginterview.com/resources,* a web site that supplements this book. The rating processes should enable you to clearly realize the strengths and weaknesses of these sample responses. After this practice applying your knowledge and understanding of the *Winning Interview 9*, the next step is critical. You watch the video recording of your *cold interview* and then analyze it using the ratings. Your notes and use of rating categories during this analysis will give you a clear sense of your strengths, as well as your needs, as you prepare for your actual interview. In turn, while you consider your strengths and areas for improvement, you will begin to prepare for a second mock interview which you will also video record.

To train for your second mock interview, you will complete specific tasks including communication-building activities and a thorough research of your potential employer. Once you have completed your second mock interview and again used the rating criteria, you should realize your tremendous progress as compared to your *cold interview.* Most importantly, you should be empowered with strategies that capitalize on your strengths and effectively address your needs in preparation for your actual interview. As a result, you should be well on your way to winning your interview!

The Winning Interview Process – Basic Steps

Understand Interview Formats

⇩

Review Interviewing Basics: Checklists to References

⇩

Prepare a List of the Questions that May Be Asked In Your Interview

⇩

Video Your First Mock Interview – Your *Cold Interview*

⇩

Learn the *Winning Interview 9*

⇩

Watch and Analyze Sample Interview Responses

⇩

Analyze and Chart Your *Cold Interview*

⇩

Train for Your Second Mock Interview

⇩

Video and Analyze Your Second Mock Interview

⇩

Final Preparations

Small Investment – Big Reward

Reading this book and completing the entire process can be accomplished in a weekend. The quality of your results will largely depend on your commitment and focus. The allotment of time and energy will be a small price to pay for the job you are seeking.

When you consider the time of a weekend compared to other efforts you have made to build your career, the return on investment is exceptional. Think about the hours, days, and weeks you spent in high school trying to earn grades that would assure your admission to college. In addition, perhaps you took a preparation course for the SAT or ACT; again, days and hours of work. Then, there was the huge commitment of college followed by preparation courses for perhaps the GRE, LSAT or the MCAT. Next, you may have spent years developing a favorable reputation as an entry-level employee. However, once you are facing the milestones in your career, the crucible for all of these preparations and experiences is the interview. Within twenty to forty minutes, critical decisions are made about your future. Using a relatively small amount of time and making the commitment to be well-prepared for your interview can provide a remarkably high return for your investment.

Summary and First Tasks

In summary, this book is intended to lead you to:

- thoughtfully and thoroughly prepare for your pending job interview
- role play and reflect about your interviewing strengths as well as your needs
- master strategies that will empower you to capitalize on your strengths and address your needs
- walk into your interview with a level of confidence and preparation that would be unlikely without the *Winning Interview* process.

As you work through the *Winning Interview* tasks, you should develop an enhanced ability to communicate your knowledge, skills, and talents, and most importantly, an enhanced ability to communicate your personal strengths; the strengths that can set you apart from other candidates and lead you to win your job.

To begin the *Winning Interview* process, your first task is to create and complete your own mock interview. To help you prepare, you need to complete a *Pre-Interview Questionnaire*. It will lead you to create questions and scenarios that anticipate and simulate your actual upcoming job interview.

You will video record your responses and performance and thereby establish your *cold interview*. It becomes the baseline of your interviewing skills. Let's begin. The *Pre-Interview Questionnaire* is on the next page.

Winning Interview

Pre-Interview Questionnaire

First Mock Interview

Name of Potential Employer: _____

Date of Upcoming Interview: _____

Time: _____   **Location:** _____

Position Title: _____

Possible Questions:

1. Tell us about yourself and why you are interested in joining our organization.*

2.

3.

4.

5.

6.

7.

8.

* This is one of the most common questions in an interview. It is included for your mock interviews, because even if it isn't asked, preparation of a response provides you stronger readiness. For example, your interviewers may request that you provide an opening statement. If so, you have a clear and organized response in mind, rather than randomly searching your mind and grasping for bits of information regarding your experiences and skills. Also, there is an opportunity in most interviews to offer a concluding statement. If so, preparation of a response to this question helps you be ready.

Your First Mock Interview - The Cold Interview

When you have completed the *Pre-Interview Survey,* you are ready for your first mock interview. This *cold interview* establishes the baseline for measuring your progress as you use the *Winning Interview* process.

Enlist the help of a friend or relative to act as your potential employer and ask you the questions for this interview. You should select a space and time that will be uninterrupted for about 35 minutes. Use a video camera that will allow you to review the interview on either your computer or video player. Respond to each of the questions from your *Pre-Interview Survey* as you would in your upcoming interview. Refrain from stops and re-dos, since they are not options in a real interview.

Chapter II
The Basics

Overview – The Basics

This chapter provides a brief review of the interview processes and formats that are typically used by organizations to select candidates. A general understanding of the possible scenarios that you may encounter should increase your interviewing skills and confidence. The chapter also discusses references and portfolios. It concludes with tasks and checklists that also will help you prepare for your interview.

Interview Formats

Interviews can take many forms. This section reviews a variety of interview formats. The premise is that familiarity with the basic types of interviews will help you feel more capable and self-assured in the varied situations that you may encounter. Typically, business, educational, government, and non-profit organizations rely on a combination of interview formats to screen and select job candidates. The formats range from the typical structured interview, to behavioral interviews, to the *let's chat and see if you and I are compatible* interview. The first interview format that is discussed is the screening interview.

Preliminary Screening Interviews / Rating Scales

Organizations that have large numbers of job applicants often use a preliminary telephone interview or a timed internet interview designed to screen for the most promising candidates. To move forward in the selection process, job candidates must be successful with the screening interview. Questions during a screening interview may come at the candidate in rapid succession.

As an example, the question on the phone or that appears on the internet may ask the candidate to respond to a prompt, such as:

I work up to my potential:

40% of the time

60% of the time

whenever the opportunity is available

100% of the time.

Thinking through such prompts to derive the *right answer* can be problematic. A candidate who is currently underemployed or unemployed may initially think to answer, *whenever the opportunity is available.* However, the answer that will earn the most points on the screening device is *100% of the time.*

These researched-based screening procedures assign ratings to responses, and the results determine if the candidate moves to the next level of interviewing. Typically, the ratings are tallied in a variety of categories, such as *work ethic*, *group compatibility*, and *career commitment.* The example provided above would be a *work ethic* prompt. The idea is to create a profile of the strengths and weaknesses of a job candidate.

The screening interviews also may be testing the candidates for basic skills that are required to perform the job. These performance tests may be evaluating candidates' math skills or writing abilities or knowledge of software programs. Those candidates who do well with the screening questions and performance tests may then be scheduled for a case interview or an actual personal interview as the next step.

Traditional Interviews or Structured Interviews

Traditionally, employers have relied on a set list of questions to evaluate job candidates. These structured questions are intended to give job candidates the opportunity to discuss their skills, experience, and knowledge for the range of qualifications that are required by the job. Many interview preparation books focus primarily on structured interviews. In reality, however, few employers rely only on traditional interview methods when selecting candidates. Many also include behavioral questions and targeted tests of skills as part of their interviewing procedures. *Winning Interview* prepares job candidates for a wide range of interview formats.

Simulation Interviews / Case Interviews

Simulation scenarios, or case interviews, place the interviewee in a situation that is similar to the everyday demands of the job or ask candidates how they have handled a given situation in the past. The purpose is to determine how potential employees behave in an actual job environment. Hence, these interviews are also known as behavioral or situational interviews. In the simplest form, a case interview may take the form of behavioral questions embedded within a structured interview. For example, candidates may be asked a question such as, "What is the most significant time-management challenge that you have faced and how did you handle it?"

At a more complex level, the case interview may place candidates in a simulated job scenario. As an example, a candidate who is applying to be trained as an investment counselor for a large investment fund might be asked to phone potential clients. These clients, who are actually actors, would engage in discussions about their investment goals. This mock investment discussion would take place as a conference call. Simultaneously, an interviewing panel would be listening to the conversation and rating the candidate's performance.

In another more common performance-based scenario, candidates are given data that reflect the job environment for the position they are seeking. The candidates are placed in a room with a computer and given a specified amount of time to analyze the data and develop a written prioritized plan for the department. An interview panel then analyzes and rates the plan.

Many organizations favor such simulations or case interview approaches because they can gather a sense of a candidate's ability to work under pressure, think creatively, problem solve, and generate viable ideas. Case interviews are likely to be specific to the needs of the organization, whether the field is accounting, architecture, information technology, or health management.

For these behavioral interviews, familiarity with a repertoire of strategies is helpful. If the behavioral interview takes the form of a job simulation activity, you should be focused, energized, and analytical. One of your priorities should be to determine the goals of the activity. Is it designed to test specific skills, assess your interpersonal abilities, or evaluate your problem solving strengths? As you realize the purposes of the activity, bring forth your strengths in these categories. As an example, for the investment phone simulation previously mentioned, you might realize during the simulation that one of the purposes of the activity is to test your interpersonal skills. In turn, you would project your affability, sense of humor, and ability to be a good listener.

If you are assigned a problem-solving task typical to the job that you are seeking, remember that time management is critical. Here is a step-by-step approach that works for many behavioral scenarios that require a written product:

- quickly identify what is important and relevant for the task
- use the information you have been provided in combination with what you know about the organization to quickly develop your ideas for a plan
- note your ideas in the form of key words
- number the key words to create an organized and coherent flow for the ideas
- begin writing or word processing your plan
- leave at least three minutes for proofreading and corrections at the end of the session.

Roughly, a candidate's time for a thirty-minute job simulation can be divided into seven minutes for absorbing and analyzing, three minutes for generating ideas and notes, seventeen minutes for writing, and three minutes for proofreading and correcting.

After completing a behavioral scenario, you may be asked to explain it and defend it to an interview panel, or the panel may take your work and consider it separately and proceed with a conventional component of the interview.

Rating scales are commonly used during behavioral interviews as they are with screening interviews. However, in actual practice, when a candidate is interviewing with people versus internet software or a phone-prompt program, the interviewers are garnering a holistic impression of a candidate. A candidate's overall impression may ultimately have more impact on the interviewers, and hence hiring decisions, than the research-based rating procedures.   The *Winning Interview* process prepares you to do well with rating scales and also to present a favorable holistic impression.

Stress Interviews

Job candidates seldom encounter stress interviews, but those who do are much more likely to perform successfully if they understand their purpose. Stress interviews are most common in organizations with employees who must have security clearances, but they also may be used by employers that need people with strong public relations skills. Therefore, the interviews are designed to reveal candidates' security clearance issues or to test candidates' behaviors in difficult interpersonal situations.

As an example, for a stressful public relations position, a scenario may place a job candidate in a simulation with multiple oppositional clients who are making unreasonable demands. The purpose is to observe the strategies the candidate uses, or fails to use, to diffuse the situation. Your goal in this behavioral scenario would be to realize the purpose of the activity and then to project your matching skills; in this instance, patience, attentiveness, and acknowledgement of the clients' concerns coupled with an ability to re-direct the clients to an acceptable resolution Successful implementation of this approach would evidence your competency for the position.

Security-related stress interviews may ask candidates a battery of questions while they are monitored by a polygraph. At some point, candidates may be told they are untruthful, even if their responses are honest. After more accusations and uncomfortable and intrusive questions, the session may be ended, and then the candidate may be asked to return to re-do the test and again be told that the truth is necessary for the job.

This type of security stress interview is intended to cause people to reveal undisclosed situations from their past, a primary goal of the technique. For example, candidates may eventually acknowledge that they had a pen pal who lived in an enemy country or that they forged a name to pick up a prescription. More serious revelations are the ones that are likely to thwart the security clearance.

As with other types of stress interviews, stay calm and try to discern the purpose of the scenario; then, respond appropriately to that purpose. If acquiring the job is important to you, control your emotions and avoid anger or defensive behavior.

Interview Formats / Size of Organization

Generally, employers rely on multiple interviewing formats to determine the qualifications and personal characteristics of job candidates. The use and complexity of the formats may vary in relation to the size of the organization. Due to legal considerations regarding consistency, interviews in organizations of all sizes should include a common core of questions and activities that are the same for all candidates. The consistency shields the organization from accusations of unfairness and discrimination.

With small organizations, interviews may be more informal and less scripted. These employers often use a structured interview format. The interview consists of a list of questions that seek information about the candidate's experience and knowledge. A few behavioral questions may be included, for example: *What is the most challenging* Request for Proposal *that you have encountered and how did you deal with it?*

As a supplement to the interview, the employer may target specific skills or expertise needed by the organization with performance tests, perhaps assessments of word processing abilities or software knowledge. *Getting to know you* conversations are more likely to be part of the interview, since the person conducting the interview may work directly with the potential employee. *Winning Interview* helps you prepare for both structured interviews and the behavioral questions that are typically used by small organizations.

Larger organizations often determine their questions based on specific performance categories. The categories may be directly related to the evaluation procedures used throughout the organization and include topics such as *client satisfaction*, *sales performance*, or *human relations skills*. In turn, the interview questions, screening processes, or simulated job activities are intended to represent the same performance criteria used to evaluate current employees. The format may include a panel of interviewers or a one-on-one interview with a human resources specialist from the organization. The use of evaluation categories in combination with performance tests, case interviews, and traditional interviews is common in larger organizations.

The largest corporations and organizations typically use the most complex interviewing formats. In addition to interview questions directly related to an organization's evaluation procedures, the organization may hire a research firm to validate candidates' responses to questions and also to formulate and validate the questions themselves. For example, for an accounting position, managers and accountants within the organization might develop a list of characteristics that describe their most outstanding co-workers. The research firm would then create behavioral scenarios and questions that would allow these characteristics to be demonstrated during the interview procedures. The research firm would validate these questions and simulation situations by testing them with employees within the organization to see if the processes actually identify the most effective employees. The goal is for the research-based procedures to accurately select those candidates who will perform as well as the organization's most successful employees.

The strategies and protocols developed by these research firms for selecting candidates result in interview formats that are significantly more complex than solely responding to informational and behavioral questions. The selection process may include a combination of screening procedures, performance tests, written and analytical assignments, and simulations all designed to select the best candidate. As candidates complete the scenarios, their behaviors and responses are rated on the specified qualities derived from the best employees within the organization. After the candidate completes the process, the ratings are tallied and converted to a recommendation, such as *definitely hire*, *strong candidate*, *marginal candidate*, or *not recommended*.

However, as discussed earlier, once a candidate has moved to the level of a personal interview, the rating scales may have less influence. The interviewing panel will garner a holistic view of the candidate during the personal interview, and this holistic view may in actual practice be the decisive factor in determining the candidate who is selected for the position.

References

Planning for interviews should include contacting work colleagues, managers, and former teachers to request recommendations. These references should be selected thoughtfully and then provided with the courtesy of advanced notice. They should be listed with their contact information on both your application and your resume. You should refrain from the common practice of stating, *References upon Request*, since this is a roadblock to efficiently vetting a potential employee, and therefore, may cause dismissal from consideration.

At your actual interview, you should be prepared to provide your interviewers with more detailed information about each reference. For example, which reference has particular knowledge about your attributes, your character, your field of expertise, or your management ability? Also, as appropriate, you may decide to provide notes, letters, or quotes from your references. Offering additional reference information can strengthen your close of an interview and make a positive *last impression.*

Portfolios

Sharing and discussing portfolios during interviews has been a long-standing practice in many fields. Photographers, artists, and models traditionally have attended interviews with carefully prepared portfolios. The practice is increasingly common in other fields. Architects, journalists, and teachers are examples of job candidates who have learned that sharing portfolios of their work can strengthen their interview. Your research into the culture of your potential employer should include consideration of the possible role of portfolios.

For promotion within, many organizations now require that their employees develop portfolios of their work. Establishing and maintaining a file that catalogues your accomplishments is a practical career strategy. If needed, the contents of the file can readily be developed into a career portfolio and even made available to potential employers via the internet or a flash drive.

What Does the Internet Tell about You?

Another important preparation for your interview is to consider the electronic information about you that may be readily available via the internet. Is that information positive? Does it present you in the best light? Are there notable recognitions that can be found which highlight awards or career accomplishments? In contrast, is there information available that is less than favorable? If so, it can sabotage the best of interviews, references, and portfolios. Therefore, an important step in preparing for your interview is to be certain that potentially damaging information about you is cleared. This information can range from your comments on blogs, to your entries on social network sites, to your tweets. Remember that a friend can post a picture of you and then caption that picture with your name, so you need to consider what others may have posted about you as well as your own postings. What may appear funny and light-hearted on an internet social site can thwart your job prospects.

Human resource managers who use internet search engines to vet potential job candidates report that they eliminate more than thirty percent of potential employees. Be certain that what is available about you portrays competence, balance, and professionalism.

Checklists

As you begin preparation for your interview, review the following two checklists. They cover many of the basics of interviewing in a quick-review format. Reading these checklists early in your preparation process should help you incorporate these basics into your interviewing strategies. In encapsulated form, these lists represent the focus of many interview preparation books. You can print the checklists at winninginterview.com/resources.

Winning Interview
Checklists - Get Ready to Be Ready!

Interview Basics

- ☐ Arrival is timely
- ☐ Handshake is confident and eye contact is good
- ☐ Responses are clear and concise with only substantiating details
- ☐ Voice is confident and audible
- ☐ Demeanor and body language are confident, yet receptive and pleasant
- ☐ Humor is used appropriately
- ☐ Grooming is impeccable, yet relaxed
- ☐ Responses incorporate evidence, examples, and stories
- ☐ Appearance is professional
- ☐ Clothing and style refrain from making a statement; for example, *I'm into punk*
- ☐ Responses demonstrate preparation, commitment, and forethought
- ☐ Interactions evidence receptiveness to supervision and growth
- ☐ Interactions demonstrate potential compatibility and camaraderie with others
- ☐ Responses are focused and directly answer the questions
- ☐ Responses evidence knowledge of the organization, its goals, and its mission
- ☐ Attitude is positive
- ☐ Never take over an interview

General Interview Strategies

- Know the time and location of the interview.
- Travel to the interview location before the interview date to judge travel time and traffic.
- Plan to arrive fifteen minutes before the interview.
- Who will be interviewing you? A panel? A human resources specialist? A potential colleague?
- Will you be expected to participate in a simulated activity or a performance test?
- Is this a screening interview or an interview that could lead directly to a job offer?
- Dress professionally even if the organization has a business casual policy.
- Refrain from exaggeration with your clothes, tie, hair, or accessories.
- Project body language that is relaxed, attentive, and receptive.
- Use a pleasant and confident tone of voice.
- Know the organization and its web site. Do an internet search for news articles that may be relevant.
- Know your resume, including your strengths and your areas for growth.
- Be prepared to share an opening statement and a closing statement in case the opportunities are offered.
- Be prepared with questions that demonstrate your interest in the position and your knowledge of the mission of the company.
- Know the key contact person regarding the interview.
- Send the contact person a thank you note / follow-up letter immediately after the interview with a focus on your interest, enthusiasm, and matching qualities. An email format is OK for some organizations.
- Make notes after you leave the interview. What were the key questions? What were your impressions? What did you do well? How could you improve?
- Follow-through on requests, including contact a manager, send a transcript, fax a certification.

Chapter III
The Winning Interview Nine

The Key Elements

In Chapter II, you gained an understanding of interview formats, and you reviewed interview basics. The next step in preparing to analyze your first mock interview is to learn how you can set yourself apart from all other candidates. A basic premise of *Winning Interview* is that interviewers are influenced by the personal strengths that candidates project, or fail to project, during an interview. Therefore, successful communication of these positive characteristics, the *Winning Interview 9*, is likely to determine the candidate who is hired. To be the selected candidate, you need to become familiar with these nine important qualities and thereby increase your success in projecting these personal strengths during your interview.

The Winning Interview 9

Training, Experience, and Knowledge

Job candidates customarily give this category the most attention as they prepare for their interview. However, there may be few or no questions directly related to your training, experience, and knowledge during your interview. The reason is that your resume and any preliminary screening instruments, such as a phone interview or performance activity, are likely to have determined your baseline qualifications. The interviewers are already satisfied that you are capable of fulfilling the essential requirements of the position. Now they are looking for other indications that you will make a significant contribution to the organization.

However, if you are asked questions in this category, you must be prepared with strong responses. Also, expect that questions may be behavioral. As previously discussed, behavioral questions require that you use your expertise and knowledge to solve a potential job challenge or ask you to explain how you solved a job challenge in the past. To showcase your qualifications for all types of questions, be prepared with responses that include these three components:

1. Highlights of your training, experience, knowledge
2. Examples of how you have effectively used that training, experience, knowledge
3. Examples of how your training, experience, knowledge will be valuable to the organization.

Your responses in this category are your opportunity to demonstrate that your skills are a unique match for the organization's needs. Sample question: *We know that your present employer simultaneously won multiple U.S. government contracts. As a member of your employer's human resources team, what were the personnel challenges that you faced and how did you resolve them?*

Energy

Employers seek to hire candidates that bring positive energy and collegial synergy to their organization. How can you convey that you will enthusiastically contribute to the organization, its environment, and its culture? Rather than asking a specific question for this category, interviewers are likely to gather a general impression of your positive, versus flat or negative energy, based on your demeanor and attitude during the interview. Sample question: *On a scale of 1-10 rate your efficiency in completing tasks. Explain your rating.*

Innovation

Organizations are often looking for employees who will bring more current expertise to their operation. Do you have cutting-edge training and experience in your field? Are you a recent graduate who has been trained in the latest technologies and practices? This category gives you the opportunity to demonstrate how you can help the organization maintain or attain status as a leader in current and innovative practices. Questions for this category are likely to specifically relate to your area of expertise. Be prepared to provide examples. Sample question: *Our field managers request accounting data in Excel. Do you have experience interfacing MS Query and Excel?*

Compatibility

In today's work environments, employees are often part of a team. Consequently, many employers seek employees who are flexible yet productive contributors to team efforts. How do you handle a co-worker who shirks responsibility on a team? Do you initiate tasks within a team or only follow? Do you attempt to dominate a team or serve only as a contributor? Responses to questions related to this category can be a delicate balance. A potential team member may be on your interview panel and may be the team leader. If so, the leader will be looking for a contributor to the team in terms of skills, ideas, affability, and initiative but may be threatened by a potentially dominant team member. Therefore, to successfully demonstrate compatibility, you need to convey during the interview that you are a contributor and that you also are open to guidance and supervision. Sample question: *We are looking for a candidate that will become part of a five- person team. What can team members expect from you?*

Commitment

In this category, employers are looking for your willingness to obligate your time and energy to the goals of the organization. How can you convey that you will be a dedicated and loyal employee? Be prepared to explain your willingness to get done what needs to be done. Think of examples from your career that demonstrate your job commitment. Be ready to share these examples. Sample question: *Sometimes deadlines approach, and there seems to be more to do than can be done. How do you handle such situations?*

Initiative

Employers are more likely to hire candidates who demonstrate initiative. Do you languish without focus until you are given directions, or do you finish tasks and identify what needs to be done next? Do you offer ideas for improvement and innovation? *Initiative* is another personal characteristic that should be carefully balanced in an interview. You need to be ready to demonstrate your initiative, yet also prepared to demonstrate a willingness to readily respond to supervision and the leadership of others. Sample question: *Can you tell us about a time when you made a positive difference for your present organization?*

Ego Strength

Employees who have a strong belief in their capabilities, knowledge, and skills can be especially valuable to an organization. Such individuals see their performance as a reflection of who they are. They want to be known as a competent person who meets deadlines, leads others, and solves problems. Such employees are important role models to others in the organization. Can you share an example of colleagues turning to you for assistance? Employees with ego strength define themselves by being known for doing their job very well. Sample question: *What are four of your professional strengths? How do those strengths make a positive difference for your employer?*

Mission

Individuals with a sense of mission have thoughtfully considered their future and established long-term goals. Valuable employees align their personal career goals with the goals and mission of the organization. Their job performance is motivated by a strong determination to attain their defined personal goals. Sample question: *Where do you see yourself five years from now?*

Vision

The most sought-after and valuable organizational leaders are able to gather input and information from the employees, practices, and goals of an organization and then create multiple, original, and varied ideas. When this process is accomplished effectively, the result is vision. A leader who can create a viable vision for an organization can contribute immensely to that organization's advancement. Vision also is a product of a leader's ability to think beyond the commonplace. Leaders with vision seek alternative approaches and are willing to test them. Can you assess the common practices of the organization and change and elaborate them in beneficial ways? A leader with marketable vision must have sound judgment. They must be able to discern those ideas that are realistic and practical for the organization versus those that would sidetrack and weaken the organization. Sample question: *What is a significant need that exists in your current company? How could addressing that need make a positive and significant difference for the company's future?*

Apply Your Knowledge
of the Winning Interview 9

In the next chapter, you will strengthen your understanding and mastery of the *Winning Interview 9* by viewing sample interview responses of candidates who communicate, or fail to communicate, the characteristics. You will be able to view the responses via the internet. This practice with evaluating the successful or unsuccessful communication of the *Winning Interview 9* should empower you to more effectively project these personal strengths during your actual interview.

Chapter IV
The Analysis

Apply – The First Look

Now that you are familiar with basic interviewing formats and the *Winning Interview 9*, you will use your knowledge to analyze sample interview responses. This practice with sample candidate responses will prepare you to analyze your first mock interview, your *cold interview*. To facilitate this process, this book provides internet access to videos of four job candidates. The first video features Jake and Jen, responding to the same interview prompt: *Tell us about yourself and why you are interested in employment with our organization.* Access the interview simulations for Jake and Jen at: *winninginterview.com/resources.* Review their responses. You may find taking notes helpful as you formulate your reactions.

The scripts for Jake's response and Jen's response are copied below:

Rating Interview Responses - I

Question: *Tell us about yourself and why you are interested in employment with our organization.*

Response - Jake: I graduated from Middleton in 2008 with a degree in IT Networking. I couldn't find an IT job in my small town, so I was working at the local Wal-Mart. A neighbor told my Dad that I should check the *Washington Post* for ads for people trained in IT. I made a couple of phone calls and came to Rockville for an interview. I landed the job with *Air Ghost.* Everything's been cool there, but I met a girl who lives in Virginia, and now, trying to see her with the commute and all is a bust. So, I want a job with your company because it'll make my life a lot simpler.

Score _____

Response - Jen: I've been working with an IT team at *Air Ghost* in Rockville since 2000. During that time, I've developed a strong networking expertise using *Cisco* products. The team that I have worked with has nicknamed me the deadline hero, because a couple of times I've used my college IT training to solve problems that were holding up the team. I'm interested in your company because you work with much larger clients, and from what I understand, a lot of your clients have special security needs. I believe I would have some great opportunities for growth with you, and at the same time I know that you primarily work with *Cisco* products, and I'm really comfortable with them.

I'm also interested in your company because the larger size will give me more opportunities for growth and advancement. I would like to develop enough expertise to manage teams within a few years. I enjoy sharing what I know. It's a good feeling when people see you as an expert!

Score _____

What Do You Think?

These two job candidates, Jake and Jen, could have similar job application and comparable resumes. Both candidates have degrees in information technology, and both may have the same number of years of experience at *Air Ghost*. However, despite equal qualifications on paper, which candidate would you hire? The responses of the two candidates present an excellent validation of the *Winning Interview Nine*. Review Jen's interview and consider how her responses communicated her positive attributes in eight of the nine *Winning Interview* categories. Below, her responses are matched with the categories to help you appreciate that a job candidate can communicate each of the *Winning Interview Nine* attributes in just a few sentences.

Training, Experience, Knowledge –
- *I've developed a strong networking expertise using* Cisco *products.*

Innovation –
- *I've used my college IT training to solve problems that were holding up the team.*

Compatibility –
- *The team that I have worked with has nicknamed me the deadline hero.*

- *I enjoy sharing what I know.*

Commitment –
- *. . .the deadline hero.*

Initiative –
- *I'm interested in your company because you work with much larger clients.*

Ego Strength –
- *I enjoy sharing what I know. It's a good feeling when people see you as an expert!*

Mission –

- *I would like to develop enough expertise to manage teams within a few years.*

- *I would have some great opportunities for growth with you, and at the same time I know that you primarily work with* Cisco *products, and I'm really comfortable with them.*

This categorization of Jen's responses is not mutually exclusive. Many of Jen's responses could fit into more than one category. However, regardless of how they are labeled, a review of Jake's responses versus Jen's responses leaves little doubt that a job candidate who can communicate the *Winning Interview* 9 is likely to be the candidate who wins the job.

Apply – A Second Look

To give you additional practice analyzing an interview response before you review your first mock interview, here are answers from two candidates to a very different interview question. The scripts for Mary's response and Mark's response are copied below and also are available at the web site: *winninginterview.com/resources* .

Rating Interview Responses - II

Question: *What do you see as the role of focus groups?*

Response – Mary: I know that *focus groups* is when people sit around and tell what they think about an idea or product. I have a friend who ran focus groups for a medical research company. I know she felt a lot of pressure, because if she was wrong about what she thought people were saying, she could lose her job.

Score: _____

Response - Mark: I've done a lot of reading and research about focus groups, and I believe the role of focus groups is critical. They can help a company decide if they are on the right track before making big investments and big mistakes. What I like about the information from focus groups is that it can be seen not so much as a determining factor in decision making, but rather as a starting point. What's good about our idea? How can we tweak it? How can we elaborate it? How can it best be marketed? What are the demographic implications for this product? Focus groups can help an organization take a good idea and make it great!

Score: _____

Mark's response for this interview question doesn't demonstrate as many of the *Winning Interview 9*, nor does it fit as easily into the categories when compared to Jen's response in the previous scenario. However, we clearly garner a sense that Mark is likely to win the interview. First, in his opening statement, Mark demonstrates that he has completed research about the company's business. In turn, he has identified focus groups as a key component of the operation, and then informed himself on the topic, and also prepared a strong response. These preparations enable Mark to provide positive communication to his interviewers about his knowledge and his professional commitment.

Also, his response illustrates that he can take his knowledge and develop an innovative perspective on a commonplace marketing research tool: *. . . it can be seen not so much as a determining factor in decision making, but rather as a starting point.* In addition, Mark's willingness to talk about his innovative perspective reflects his initiative as well as his self-confidence, or ego strength. Therefore, Mark's response has communicated positive attributes about himself as a job candidate in six of the *Winning Interview 9* categories:

Training, Experience, Knowledge –
- *I've done a lot of reading and research about focus groups . . . .*

Energy –
- *Focus groups can help an organization take a good idea and make it great!*
- Mark leans forward, he uses eye contact, his body language is attentive, and his voice is upbeat.

Innovation –
- *. . . it can be seen not so much as a determining factor in decision making, but rather as a starting point. . . .*

Commitment -
- *I've done a lot of reading and research about focus groups . . . .*

Initiative –
Mark's effort to take his knowledge about focus groups and develop a new perspective

Ego Strength –
Mark's confidence about his ideas; his willingness to share them in an interview

When we compare his communication of positives in these six categories to the lack of positives in any categories for Mary's response, we understand that Mark is clearly the candidate who is likely to win the job. Also, as discussed earlier, notice the power of the holistic impact of Mark's responses. His overall interview makes a positive and potentially decisive impression.

In addition, be aware that neither of the candidates refers to direct experience with focus groups. However, Mark knew their importance, and even though he was inexperienced with the practice, he sidestepped the potential pitfall of a response that could have eliminated him as a candidate: "Well, I've never worked with focus groups."

Apply - Analyze Your First Mock Interview

Now you should be prepared to review and analyze your *cold interview*. First, watch your entire interview. As you view it, think about your first impressions and any general patterns that emerge. Take notes on these impressions and patterns during and after watching the interview. Summarize your conclusions in a paragraph or two.

Next, watch your *cold interview* again. This time take notes using the chart on pages 46 - 49, *Written Analysis – First Mock Interview.* You can print a full-page version of the chart by accessing it via the internet at *winninginterview.com/ resources.* Stop and replay sections of the interview as needed to accurately record and develop your notes.

A review of your summary notes in combination with your more specific notes should give you a strong sense of your strengths as well as those areas that need your focus.

The next step is important. Use the rating sheets titled *Response Rating Sheet - Mock Interview I* on pages 50 and 51. They are available for printing at *winninginterview.com/resources.* For each question and each category, assign yourself a score from 1 to 10, with 10 as the most effective response for a given category. In some cases, you may need to leave the category blank because your response didn't offer an appropriate opportunity to capitalize on that category. The *Response Rating Sheet* will provide you a clear sense of your strongest responses. Look across the rows and see which questions most closely averaged a 10. For which questions did you have the lowest average scores? How will you improve your responses for those questions? Make notes to capture your ideas. These notes can serve as a guide as you practice for your *Second Mock Interview.*

Now, consider the vertical columns. Where are your strengths? Did you do well in *Commitment, Innovation,* or *Mission?* Remember, *Mission* is demonstrating that your personal goals merge with the goals of the organization. *Valuable employees align their personal sense of mission with the goals and mission of the organization.*

Where do you need to strengthen your communication about your attributes? Perhaps you need to provide your interviewers with more evidence that you are a team contributor or that you will merge comfortably with the present work team. *Employers seek to hire candidates that bring positive energy and collegial synergy to their organization.* Develop a plan to address your areas of need by making notes about possibilities for improvement. Encapsulate your ideas for improvement into key words, a few for each category. These key words can guide you as you prepare and practice for you *Second Mock Interview.* For example, if your *Energy* appeared weak during the interview, your key words might be: *enthusiasm, lean forward, eye contact, smile.*

Winning Interview
Written Analysis – First Mock Interview

Question 1:

Strengths-

Missed Opportunities –

Question 2:

Strengths-

Missed Opportunities –

Question 3:

    Strengths-

    Missed Opportunities –

Question 4:

    Strengths-

    Missed Opportunities –

Question 5:

    Strengths-

    Missed Opportunities –

Question 6:

    Strengths-

    Missed Opportunities –

Question 7:

    Strengths-

    Missed Opportunities –

Question 8:

    Strengths-

    Missed Opportunities –

Winning Interview
Response Rating Chart – Mock Interview I

Questions	Training Experience Knowledge	Energy	Innovation	Compatibility
1				
2				
3				
4				
5				
6				
7				
8				

Totals:

Questions	Commit-ment	Initiative	Ego	Mission	Vision	Totals
1						
2						
3						
4						
5						
6						
7						
8						

Totals:

Chapter V
The Second Mock Interview

Preparation

Your preparation for your second mock interview is more comprehensive than the preparation for your *cold interview*. Now you will use your interviewing knowledge as a foundation for more thoughtful and thorough planning. The categories of the *Winning Interview* 9 are revisited and explained in more detail. Specific tasks are included with the categories to help you strengthen your readiness. Mastering this chapter and completing the tasks should significantly improve your performance for your second mock interview and also significantly bolster your readiness and your confidence for your actual interview.

Training, Experience, and Knowledge

This section includes several suggestions to help you prepare for the *Training, Experience, and Knowledge* category. To begin, thoroughly familiarize yourself with the job description for the position for which you are applying. To make the position description more real for you, outline your anticipation of a typical day on the job. What would be the sequence of events during the day? What challenges would you expect? Might you have specific responsibilities as part of a workgroup? Would there be meetings and deadlines? How would you prepare for a typical day? What would you need to know? Make notes as you develop your ideas.

Now that you have a practical sense of the responsibilities of the position, the next step is to consider your strengths relative to the job. To help you realize your strengths and be prepared to communicate them, reflect about what you do well in your current position or in situations similar to the job description. Create lists that describe your strengths and then summarize them with specific examples and key words.

The next preparation task is to correlate your knowledge of the position with your strengths. Where are the matches? Might any of your strengths be the key asset that your potential employer is seeking? Remember Jen's simulated interview response: *I've developed a strong networking expertise using Cisco products.* What are the contributions that you can offer for the job you are seeking? Be prepared to highlight these potential contributions during the interview, and remember that the most effective way to communicate your strengths is through concise stories and examples. You need to be prepared to explain why you will be valuable to your potential employer.

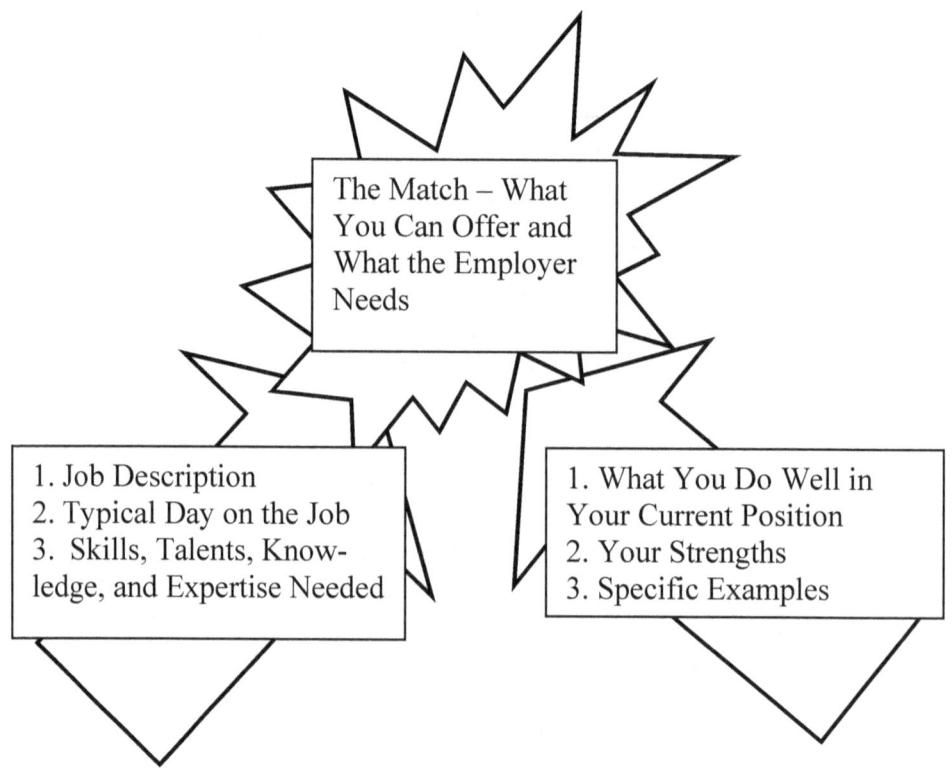

The Match – What You Can Offer and What the Employer Needs

1. Job Description
2. Typical Day on the Job
3. Skills, Talents, Knowledge, and Expertise Needed

1. What You Do Well in Your Current Position
2. Your Strengths
3. Specific Examples

Another preparation that is important for the *Training, Experience, and Knowledge* component of the *Winning Interview 9* is to consider any of your shortcomings relative to the position you are seeking. During your interview, you may be asked to address these shortcomings. If so, be prepared by formulating a response that either addresses how you are capable of compensating for the shortcomings or that explains your willingness and efforts to eliminate the shortcomings through coursework, training, or more varied opportunities. Condense your response into a few key words, and plan to take these key words with you into your interview.

Now you can walk into your interview with several strong preparations in place for questions about your *Training, Experience, and Knowledge.* You are informed about the position you are seeking. You have carefully thought about your career strengths and their match to the position. You are prepared to address questions about the limitations of your qualifications relative to the position.

Energy

A red flag during any interview is a person who projects a flat and vapid level of energy. Any employer will be favorably impressed by a potential employee who will bring expertise plus revitalizing energy to the organization. You should plan to project positive, upbeat, yet appropriate energy during your interview. Here are some strategies that should help.

First, review your *cold interview* and consider your voice. Does it sound positive and lively and thereby contribute energy to the interview? If not, practice adjusting your voice tone and cadence to project an appropriate level of enthusiasm.

Also, consider your ability to use humor. If you aptly capitalize on opportunities to interject humor during your interview, you will project positive energy. Humor can also help relax you and the people who are interviewing you.

Another key component of *Energy* is body language. Research affirms that body language is a primary communicator in interpersonal settings. Therefore, your non-verbal signals during an interview are critical for your success. What were you communicating during your *cold interview*? When questions were asked, did you lean forward and listen carefully to indicate your commitment and interest? With your interviewer, did you make and vary eye contact to demonstrate that you were attentive? Did you smile appropriately to show a positive and upbeat disposition? The best interview answers can be lost on your audience if your body language indicates a cold, distant, or insecure demeanor, thus communicating lackluster or negative energy.

You can also convey energy during your interview by sharing your contributions to positive team dynamics. When has your encouragement, or perhaps your sense of humor, caused enthusiasm to build among your colleagues? Have you organized a deadline or a request for proposal into a game among your co-workers? Be ready to share an anecdote that communicates your energizing influence on your work environment.

Innovation

Your ability to demonstrate *Innovation* can be decisive in convincing your interviewers that you are the best match for the job. How might the organization become more successful because of your expertise, experiences, creativity, and problem solving? Do you have training that is cutting edge? Has the organization won a new contract and therefore needs your expertise? Review the list of strengths that you prepared previously, and identify those attributes that may be especially valuable to the organization in terms of innovation and current knowledge. Then be ready to provide specific examples of how you have used your expertise to innovate and resolve problems. Remember Jen's response when she said, . . . *a couple of times I've used my college IT training to solve problems that were holding up the team.* Preparation of just a few relevant phrases can be powerful. Be ready to explain your strengths as an innovator.

Compatibility

As we discussed in our initial review of the *Winning Interview 9,* many workplaces rely on teams of employees to meet deadlines and achieve goals. Therefore, selecting job candidates who will work effectively with co-workers is often a high priority for employers.

Recall that Jen's response addressed compatibility: *The team that I have worked with has nicknamed me the deadline hero.* To help you prepare responses that communicate compatibility, reflect on your work experiences with groups. What are positives that your co-workers might say about you? List these positives. Be prepared to speak to these strengths with specific examples, comments, or even by sharing copies of emails and notes.

Also, in case you are asked, be prepared to discuss suggestions for improvement that colleagues or a former manager might have given you. Honest self-evaluation is a valuable characteristic of a good employee. Can you take suggestions for improvement and make them into positives? If you can share an example of this trait, you can demonstrate your openness to direction and hence, your compatibility. Here is an example:

> *My colleagues used to consider me impatient. There is some accuracy in that perspective. I have always been focused on getting the job done. Over time, however, I have learned to turn my impatience into encouragement. I regularly check with my co-workers about their progress and encourage them. Now, rather than being tagged as impatient, I think my co-workers see me as a bit of a cheerleader.*

Notice that a potentially negative attribute is stated to highlight multiple positives. Job commitment is evidenced by the statement: *I have always been focused on getting the job done.* Flexibility is evident in the response, . . . *I have learned to turn my impatience into encouragement.* Also, positive energy and group synergy are communicated: *I think my co-workers see me as a bit of a cheerleader.* Opportunities to discuss your shortcomings during your interview can be a major plus. Be prepared.

Flexibility and openness to multiple perspectives are also important components of group compatibility. Do you know when to offer ideas and leadership? In contrast, are you willing to accept suggestions and take direction? Do you strive to help a group make a good idea better? These are all indications of a team player, a role that you need to communicate during your interview.

As you reflect about your compatibility, consider these common teamwork dilemmas:

> How do you handle a co-worker who shirks responsibility on a team?
>
> Do you initiate tasks within a team or only follow?
>
> Do you attempt to dominate a team or serve only as a contributor?

Be prepared to use your list of positive colleague comments, your self-assessment, and your thoughtful consideration of these questions to explain how you can contribute to the organization's success.

Commitment

The *Commitment* component of the *Winning Interview 9* requires that you communicate during your interview that you are willing to . . . *obligate your time and energy to the goals of the organization.*

Organizations seek employees who see their jobs as more than an income source. During your career, how have you demonstrated on-the-job commitment? Do you recall working overtime and throughout the weekend to meet a deadline? Have you taken courses to advance your career? Do you hold certifications that evidence your willingness to improve your expertise? Again, as previously discussed, a short anecdote is the best way to communicate that you are an employee who is dedicated to getting the job done. Have your example of commitment ready to share during your interview.

Initiative

During your interview, you need to provide evidence that you are a person with initiative. Recall Jake's response in his simulated interview:

> *A neighbor told my Dad that I should check the* Washington Post *for ads for people trained in IT.*

Here's an example of a person who not only is failing to score points in one of the *Winning Interview 9* categories, but actually may be moving into the negative column. He is telling his prospective employer that he lacked the initiative to seek a job beyond being a stock boy; that a push from his neighbor and his Dad was the reason he made a change.

To avoid Jake's situation, be prepared to demonstrate your initiative during your interview. Perhaps you have encouraged and led your colleagues to convert to a new software platform? Have you made a suggestion to your present employer that improved procedures? Have you identified best practices and discussed them with co-workers? Make a few notes so you are ready to explain that you use your initiative to make positive contributions.

Ego-Strength

Good employees believe that they are capable of doing their jobs and those who are organizational leaders need strong self-confidence when faced with difficult decisions and challenging situations. As explained in the initial definition of *Ego Strength,* good employees identify with their career performance:

> *Employees who have a strong belief in their capabilities, knowledge, and skills . . . see their performance as a reflection of who they are. They want to be known as the person who is competent . . . who is a leader . . . .*

How can you communicate during your interview that you believe in yourself and your capabilities? Be prepared to explain why you are a strong and competent leader. Do you have leadership roles in professional organizations? Have your present managers asked you to take the lead on a project or to solve a challenge? Do your colleagues look to you for guidance and support? Think of specific success stories and be prepared to share your belief in your capabilities.

Mission

One of your primary focuses for interview preparation should be the *Mission* category of the *Winning Interview 9:*

> *Individuals with a sense of mission maintain their immediate and long-term goals as a high priority. Valuable employees align their personal sense of mission with the goals and mission of the organization. Their performance is motivated by strong determination to attain defined personal goals.*

Recall that Jen aligned her personal mission with the mission of her potential employer:

I would have some great opportunities for growth with you, and at the same time I know that you primarily work with Cisco products, and I'm really comfortable with them.

The implication for your upcoming interview is that you need to thoroughly know the mission, goals, and culture of your potential employer. Research the organization's web site. Seek out any contacts that you may have who work for the organization and ask them to share their perspectives. Consider using professional networking web sites such as *LinkedIn* to access contacts that may offer you inside perspectives. Check web resources such as *Yahoo Financial* for current economic news about the organization. Consider these questions:

Who are the organization's principal clients?
What contracts have recently been won?
What does the organization value, and how can you contribute?
What are the vision and immediate goals of the organization's principal leaders?

To further strengthen your preparation, consult web sites that specialize in providing job applicants with information about potential employers, for example, *Vault.com*. These sites provide resources that vary from questions that were asked in previous interviews to employees' ratings of workplace environments. Although the sites usually have information available only for larger organizations and may charge a membership fee, you may decide that they are worthwhile despite the cost and limitations.

Once you have gathered a strong sense of the organization, outline your immediate and long-term career goals. How can you merge those goals with the goals of your potential employer? Develop a few sentences that will communicate during your interview that you and the organization are mutually valuable to one another.

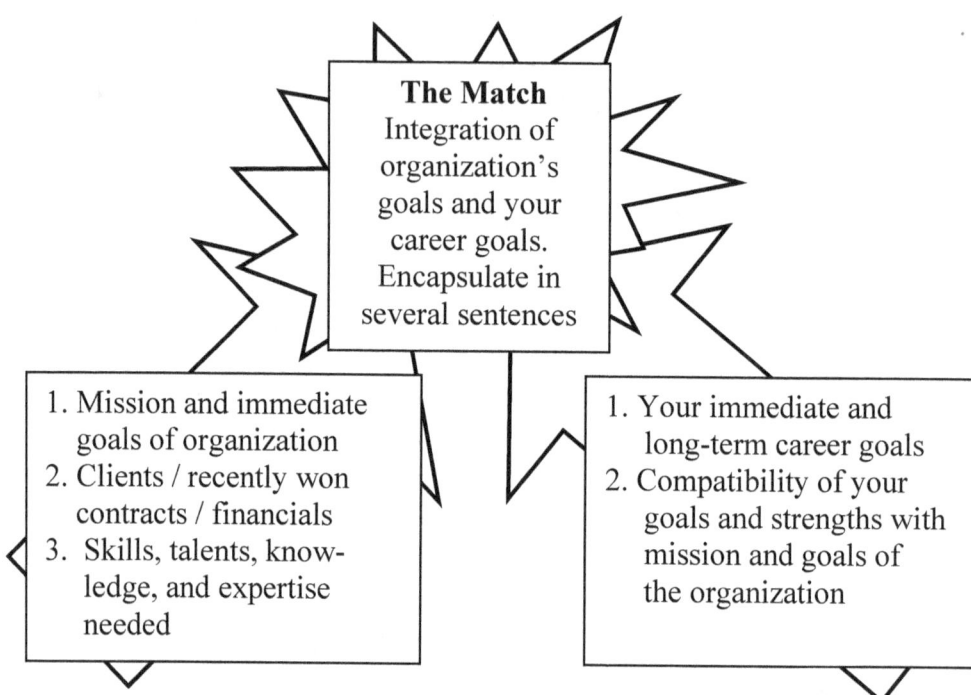

The Match
Integration of organization's goals and your career goals. Encapsulate in several sentences

1. Mission and immediate goals of organization
2. Clients / recently won contracts / financials
3. Skills, talents, knowledge, and expertise needed

1. Your immediate and long-term career goals
2. Compatibility of your goals and strengths with mission and goals of the organization

This chart represents your preparation for *Mission*. Completing the process should increase your interviewing confidence and also your readiness to explain that you are the job candidate who can best serve the organization.

Vision

The ability to garner vision is a critical element of strong leadership. This component of the *Winning Interview 9* is especially important for applicants who are seeking executive positions. *Vision* is a complex combination of many career components. Leaders who can create vision for an organization need expertise and experience in their field. They need to be effective communicators with employees at all levels of the organization. They need to know how to seek and incorporate employees' ideas and suggestions. These leaders also need to be able to analyze and validate that input as well as statistical and financial data to determine trends, implications, and courses of action. When leaders can effectively combine their knowledge and experience with exceptional analytical and communication skills, they can generate multiple, original, and varied ideas that foster the mission, needs, and culture of the organization. In turn, they can forge a vision that significantly advances the organization. What notable contributions have you made during your career? What channels of communication have you found to be especially helpful for gathering useful information? How have you advanced the mission of the organizations for which you have worked? Can you distinguish an idea that is a potential liability versus and an idea that will revitalize the organization? Be ready to share your success stories.

Pre-Interview Questionnaire – Greater Depth

Now that you have again reviewed the Winning Interview 9 and completed a variety of preparation tasks, you should complete your Pre-Interview Questionnaire for your second mock interview. This questionnaire has more categories than the one for your first mock interview. In addition, you should strive to develop more complex questions. Remember that interviewers frequently ask behavioral questions; questions that place you in a scenario and ask you how you would respond or how you have responded in the past.

Sample Questions

To help you develop better questions, samples from multiple fields that range from maritime engineering to education to telecommunications are included on the following pages. The questions also are varied to be appropriate for positions from entry-level to management. The questions begin on the next page.

Satellite Telecommunications

Management

1. How do you see current technological innovations and pending governmental policies affecting the satellite industry during the next five years?

2. What is your experience with building management teams? What combination of talents do you look for?

3. How have your expertise and previous experiences positively impacted market penetration and market share?

4. What is your approach to contract bidding? Have there been times that you have won business outside of conventional contract bidding processes?

5. Here is a scenario involving competing interests: Contractors, production managers, engineers, and designers assigned to a project repeatedly contact you with conflicting advice regarding a particular satellite design element. How would you handle the situation?

6. You could bring a range of qualifications, knowledge, skills, and experiences to this position. Share with us an example of how you have used these talents in the past to make a unique contribution to the satellite industry.

7. Innovation and cutting-edge knowledge are critical to the commercial satellite field. Talk to us about your qualifications related to innovation and cutting-edge knowledge.

8. Interactions with principals in a variety of agencies within the U.S. government and also with legislators can be an asset in this position. How comfortable are you in accessing appropriate contacts within the U.S. government?

School System Math Coordinator

Education - Management

1. What do you see as the role of the Math Instructional Coordinator with regard to minority achievement?

2. One of the primary duties of a Math Instructional Coordinator is to provide staff development. What models of staff development delivery would you use to reach the thousands of teachers in our school system? Which delivery models do you think are the most effective?

3. Often math instructional curriculum must be modified to address the needs of special populations, including ESOL, special education, and highly advanced students. What types of curriculum adaptations must be made, and how can teachers be helped to use these adaptations effectively?

4. How would you respond to a high school principal who sought your advice regarding parental concerns about the school's scheduling software because it would not assign ninth grade students to Algebra II?

5. The Math Instructional Coordinator often designs and creates curriculum as part of a team. What are your strengths and your needs as a team leader and as a team member?

6. Effective vertical integration of curriculum is a primary goal of this school system's Instructional Services Department. How would you facilitate this integration in your role as Math Instructional Coordinator?

7. How have you recently advanced your professional growth? What are your future plans for professional growth?

8. How should mathematics curriculum be assessed to determine its effectiveness?

Maritime Administration - U.S. Government Management

1. One of our challenges at the Maritime Administration is to insure that the United States shipping industry is competitive in the world market and at the same time responsive to environmental concerns. How would your expertise and experiences assist us with this challenge?

2. This position requires working with situations that sometimes involve competing stakeholders. Contractors, engineers, and designers will contact you and advocate for their particular interests. How would you handle these competing demands?

3. You have a range of qualifications, knowledge, skills, and experience that you can bring to this position. Share with us an example of how you have used these talents to solve a unique problem in the maritime industry.

4. This position will involve working collaboratively with project managers throughout the Maritime Administration. Tell us how people who have worked with you in the past would describe your strengths. What suggestions for improvement might they make?

5. This position requires interactions with a variety of agencies within the U.S. government, for example, the Department of Homeland Security and the U.S. Coast Guard. What is your experience with accessing the appropriate contacts within various governmental agencies?

6. Cross-functional knowledge of the maritime industry is important for success in this position. Citing examples, explain to us how you would apply your expertise and experiences to be successful.

Sales – Experienced

1. Share with us a time when you used a creative sales approach and it didn't work. What did you do to re-group?

2. What is your level of comfort with technology, and how do you use it to improve your job performance?

3. What are the basics that should be considered when preparing a sales presentation?

4. Where would you like your career in sales to lead – say five years from now?

5. What strategies do you use in dealing with difficult questions when you are trying to close a sale?

6. Describe a time when you led a group of people. What were the challenges you faced and how did you address those challenges?

7. What are your strengths and how will you use those strengths in our organization?

8. Talk with us about this statement, "Good companies meet market demands. Great companies create markets."

Human Resources – Entry Level

1. What innovative HR practices might you bring to our company?

2. Human resource specialists sometimes deal with difficult situations and employees who become difficult. What strategies do you use when interacting with someone who is upset?

3. What is your level of comfort with technology, and how do you use it to improve your job performance?

4. Human resource employees sometimes encounter situations when there is suddenly more to be done than seems possible. What strategies might be helpful when this happens?

5. Organization is critical in a human resource setting. What organizational tools and strategies have you used in the past?

6. Talk with us about at least three federal laws that have implications for human resource procedures and policies.

Other Resources for Job Interview Questions

For a more extensive review of job interview questions, there are many resources available in book form and also online. For a quick look at questions in book form, consider:

Hawley, Casey. <u>100+ Winning Answers to the Toughest Interview Questions</u>.

As an online resource, *Monster.com* offers a range of recommendations to help you with job interview preparation. You can find questions for a variety of fields and even simulated interviews that give you written questions and then prompt you to type your responses. Check the *Resources* section of this book for additional self-help ideas.

Complete Your Pre-Interview Questionnaire

Now that you have reviewed this sampling of questions and considered other question resources, use your ideas and what you have learned about interviewing to develop the questions for your Second Mock Interview.

Winning Interview

Pre-Interview Questionnaire

Second Mock Interview

Name of Potential Employer: _____

Date of Upcoming Interview: _____

Time: _____ **Location:** _____

Position Title and Job Description:

What have you learned about the mission, goals, and work culture of the organization from your research and networking?

What are your career goals?

How can you interrelate your career goals with the mission, goals, and work culture of your potential employer?

Possible Questions:

1. Tell us about yourself and why you are interested in joining our organization. Or, *What are your career goals? Or, Where do you see yourself five years from now? Or, Why are you a good match for our organization?*

2.

3.

4.

5.

6.

7.

8.

Your Second Mock Interview

Now that you have completed the *Pre-Interview Questionnaire* for your *second mock interview*, set aside uninterrupted time to record the interview. Again, simulate the experience as if you were in your upcoming interview. Give special focus to improving those areas that needed improvement based on your *cold interview*. Remember that your responses should be concise. Also, when possible, include specific examples; you're telling a positive story about yourself through examples. Have readily available for your *second mock interview* the resources that this book has helped you develop:

- an encapsulation of your ideas for improvement from your *cold interview*

- positive characteristics about yourself – the key words

- positive comments that co-workers offer about you

- an area for improvement that you have made positive

- an example of your initiative

- an example of your team compatibility

- your research about the organization

- your innovative knowledge or skills that the organization may need

- your career goals in support of the organization's goals.

As you complete your preparation for your *second mock interview*, keep in mind that a primary focus of the organization that is considering you as a potential employee is: *How can this candidate contribute to our organization?*

Review and Analyze Your Second Mock Interview

After you have completed your *second mock interview*, watch the recording in its entirety. Again, as you watch it, think about your first impressions and any general patterns that emerge. Take notes on these impressions and patterns during and after watching the interview. Summarize your conclusions in a paragraph or two.

As you did with your *first mock interview*, your *cold interview*, watch your *second mock interview* again. This time take notes using the following pages, *Written Analysis – Mock Interview II* which are available online for printing at: winninginterview.com/resources. Stop and replay sections of the interview as much as necessary to accurately record and develop your notes.

A review of your summary notes in combination with your more specific notes should give you a strong sense of your progress between your *first mock interview* and your *second*. Celebrate your growth and consider your areas for continuing improvement.

To analyze your situation in more detail, use the rating chart, *Response Rating Sheet - Mock Interview II*, also available online at: winninginterview.com/resources. As you did with your *First Mock Interview, assign* yourself a score from 1 to 10 for each question and each category with 10 as the most effective response. In some cases, you may need to leave a category blank, because your response didn't offer an appropriate opportunity to capitalize on the category. As with your *cold interview*, this chart should provide you a clear sense of your strongest responses. Look across the rows and see which questions most closely averaged a 10. For which questions, did you have the lowest average score? How can you improve your responses for those questions?

Next, consider the vertical columns. Where are your strengths? Have you improved your responses for

Training, Experience, and Knowledge? Remember the importance of *Mission.* You need to demonstrate that your personal goals merge with the goals of the organization: *Valuable employees align their personal sense of mission with the goals and mission of the organization.* Where do you need to better communicate your strengths? Did you adequately address shortcomings and discuss them constructively?

As you complete your analysis, choose your focus for your final interview preparations. What do you still need to improve? Should you list ideas for strengthening your responses and then do a third mock interview?

Winning Interview
Written Analysis – Second Mock Interview

Question 1:

Strengths-

Missed Opportunities –

Question 2:

Strengths-

Missed Opportunities –

Question 3:

    Strengths-

    Missed Opportunities –

Question 4:

    Strengths-

    Missed Opportunities –

Question 5:

Strengths-

Missed Opportunities –

Question 6:

Strengths-

Missed Opportunities –

Question 7:

   Strengths-

   Missed Opportunities –

Question 8:

   Strengths-

   Missed Opportunities –

Winning Interview
Response Rating Chart – Mock Interview II

Questions	Training Experience Knowledge	Energy	Innovation	Compatibility
1				
2				
3				
4				
5				
6				
7				
8				

Totals:

Questions	Commit-ment	Initiative	Ego	Mission	Vision	Totals
1						
2						
3						
4						
5						
6						
7						
8						

Totals:

Chapter VI
Final Preparations

A Three-Tiered Perspective

As you complete the *Winning Interview* process and finalize your preparations for your interview, you may find a generalized perspective regarding the *Winning Interview 9* to be helpful. The nine categories can be loosely grouped in terms of what your interviewers are seeking for various job levels. For example, if you are an entry-level candidate, the interviewers may be most swayed if you can impress them with your *knowledge and training*, your *energy*, and your ability to bring *innovation* to the organization. Your potential employer is less likely to be seeking an employee who can garner a *vision* for the organization's future. Similarly, your interviewer will be less concerned about the *ego-strength* needed to make hard decisions regarding downsizing or re-structuring the organization.

Strengths in the next three categories may be more favorably viewed by an interview panel seeking a mid-management employee. Are you compatible with the present management team - *compatibility*? Do you have a strong organizational *commitment*? Will your *initiative* result in timely task completion?

The third generalized perspective is for job candidates seeking top-level management positions. Their potential employer is most likely to focus on the last three categories of the *Winning Interview 9*. Do you believe in your capabilities enough, have the *ego-strength*, to carry out tough decisions that re-direct the organization on a better course? Is your sense of career *mission* a central focus of your life, and is it a match with the mission of the organization, such that the resulting synergy will move the organization forward? Finally, are you a person who can analyze information, communicate with employees, and incorporate goals effectively enough to create a *vision* that will lead the organization to a new and better level of performance? Obviously, an organization seeking to fill a top-level position is more interested in the candidate's strengths in these categories versus the person's knowledge and skills regarding daily operational tasks, for example, troubleshooting design issues or programming software.

Finalize Your Preparation

As you complete the *Winning Interview* process, you should realize that you are more prepared and confident for your upcoming interview. Conduct a third mock interview if you believe it will be helpful. Also, recall that on pages 26-28 there are checklists for you which highlight the basics of interview preparation. If you have the time and the inclination, there are additional interview preparation resources listed at the end of the book.

Remember that carrying notes into your interview should be OK unless you have been notified otherwise. With your notes you should include:

- An encapsulation of your ideas for improving your most recent mock interview

- An encapsulation of key words that identify your strengths

- A summary of positives based on co-workers' perspectives

- Highlights of your special skills and experiences that can help the organization innovate and address specific challenges

- An example of an area for improvement that you have addressed positively

- Any notes, emails, or evaluations that represent your strengths

- Sales records, charts, graphs, or awards that verify your accomplishments

- A summary of your career goals and their compatibility with the goals of the organization.

In addition, you should have a list of any questions that you have prepared for the interviewer. The questions should represent your interest in the job and also your knowledge of the organization and its mission.

During the Interview

As you enter the room and are introduced to those who will interview you, project a calm, pleasant, and confident demeanor. If there is an interview panel, jot their names by location at the table as they are introduced. This chart will allow you to use panel members' names if the need arises. The first few minutes of the interview are crucial, and one of your most important tasks is to establish rapport with the others in the room. Smile readily and look for opportunities to use humor appropriately; project energy. Demonstrate interest by maintaining eye contact when questions are asked and comments are shared. Keep your posture open and receptive. Leaning slightly forward from the waist will indicate interest and attentiveness. Remember to answer questions and prompts concisely and with examples. Capitalize on opportunities to make your examples into stories. Research indicates that people are more likely to listen when they are told about a situation in story form. Stay focused!

Throughout your interview, you should be comfortable with making notes as questions are asked. Take a few moments to organize your thoughts by listing key words as you formulate your responses. As needed, access the resources that you brought with you. Productive use of the seconds before you begin replying to each question should increase your confidence and also the clarity of your response.

Attempt to assess the culture that is projected by the interview panel. Is it serious? Is it informal? Strive to match what is projected, yet maintain a professional demeanor. Keep your answers honest and straightforward. Many interviewers are highly experienced in the interview setting and can readily discern less-than-honest responses.

Listen for clues during the interview about the organization's needs. Do the questions indicate that there has been conflict in the work group? Then begin to highlight your interpersonal skills. Do the questions indicate a need for particular training and expertise? Then focus on those strengths that you can offer.

Near the close of the interview, you may gather a sense of the impression you are making. Do members of the interview panel appear more relaxed? Are they smiling more? Are you invited to tour the building? Are there indications that you are being recruited?

As the interview closes, take advantage of an invitation to ask questions. Use the questions you have prepared that indicate your interest in the organization and that are based on your knowledge of the organization. What are the challenging projects on the horizon? How could you best help the present work team? Would your particular knowledge, skills, or experience be helpful? If the opportunity is offered, close your interview with a summation of your strengths that highlights your compatibility with the organization.

Refrain from asking salary questions during your interview. Salaries are best negotiated after a job offer.

Also, do your best throughout the interview, even if you decide during the interview that the job is not for you.

There is the possibility that you will be recommended to another department or that someone present in the interview will recognize your abilities and know of other opportunities that are a better match.

Good luck! Be confident and ready to win your interview!

After Your Interview

Reflect on your performance during the interview. Make notes that may be helpful in the future. Follow through with any requests for work samples, recommendations, contacts, or other information. In addition, you should contact the key person who conducted the interview with a letter that expresses your continuing interest in the position and your appreciation for the opportunity to be interviewed.

If you are not offered the position, you can request feedback about your qualifications versus the match the employer was seeking. You may also inquire about your performance during the interview. The organization may not respond to your request, but many strong human resource departments do provide feedback. The perspectives can be valuable for you next interview.

Disclaimer

The author and creator of *Winning Interview* and *winninginterview.com* recognizes that the selection of candidates for employment positions is influenced by factors outside of the job interviewing process including, but not limited to, the match between the candidate and the particular needs of the employer, the skill level of the candidate, the candidate's compatibility with potential coworkers, and salary requirements. Therefore, *Winning Interview* and *winninginterview.com* make no warranties, either expressed or implied, that the *Winning Interview* preparation process will directly or indirectly lead to obtaining an employment position.

Feedback

The *Winning Interview* team strives to provide a high-quality interview preparation process. We appreciate candid and constructive feedback. You comments can be addressed to: info@winninginterview.com. Sending comments to this email address thereby grants permission for the comments to be posted on the winninginterview.com website.

Resources

Hawley, Casey. <u>100+ Winning Answers to the Toughest Interview Questions</u>. Barron's Educational Series (2001). ISBN 0-7641-1644-4 - A concise and readable book with sample responses to a range of questions in categories that include: *Questions About Past and Current Jobs, No-Win Questions, Thorny Dilemmas, and Catch-22s.*

<u>http://career-advice.monster.com</u>
Provides links to a variety of resources for job interviews, ranging from sample questions to post-interview tasks.

<u>http://www.iona.edu/studentlife/career/students/interviewing.cfm</u>
Posted by the Career Center of Iona College. Covers the basics of a good interview. A one-stop location for links to a number of helpful web sites.

<u>http://www.rileyguide.com/netintv.html</u>
The links here cover the topics of difficult questions and also responses for job offers.

<u>http://federaljobs.net/inter.htm</u>
A promotion site for a book, but offers a good overview of the different types of interviews used for federal government positions, ranging from phone interviews to structured interviews.

<u>http://www.collegegrad.com/intv/</u>
Offers insightful advice and perspectives about job interviews. Targets the needs of recent college graduates and entry-level positions.

<u>http://www.jobfox.com/</u>
Allows you to enter specifics about your experience and skills. Then matches your qualifications to available jobs in the region of your zip code.

http://www.career.virginia.edu/students/resources/hand-outs/interviewing.pdf
Posted by the *University of Virginia Career Center.* Provides a concise yet comprehensive review of interviewing basics.

http://www.selectpro.net/
At this site you can design a behavior-based interview.

www.ingramcontent.com/pod-product-compliance
Lightning Source LLC
Chambersburg PA
CBHW071252170526
45165CB00003B/1313